Where Is Ohio?

Where Is Ohio?

by Tracy Vonder Brink

illustrated by Ted Hammond

Penguin Workshop

For my family, friends, and everyone
who calls the Buckeye State home—TVB

PENGUIN WORKSHOP
An imprint of Penguin Random House LLC
1745 Broadway, New York, NY 10019
penguinrandomhouse.com

Designed and Produced by Dinardo Design, LLC.

Library of Congress Cataloging-in-Publication Data is available.

First published in the United States of America by Penguin Workshop, 2025

Manufactured in the United States of America
CJKW

ISBN 9798217051496 (paperback)
10 9 8 7 6 5 4 3 2 1

ISBN 9798217051502 (library binding)
10 9 8 7 6 5 4 3 2 1

The authorized representative in the EU for product safety and compliance is
Penguin Random House Ireland, Morrison Chambers, 32 Nassau Street,
Dublin D02 YH68, Ireland, https://eu-contact.penguin.ie.

Contents

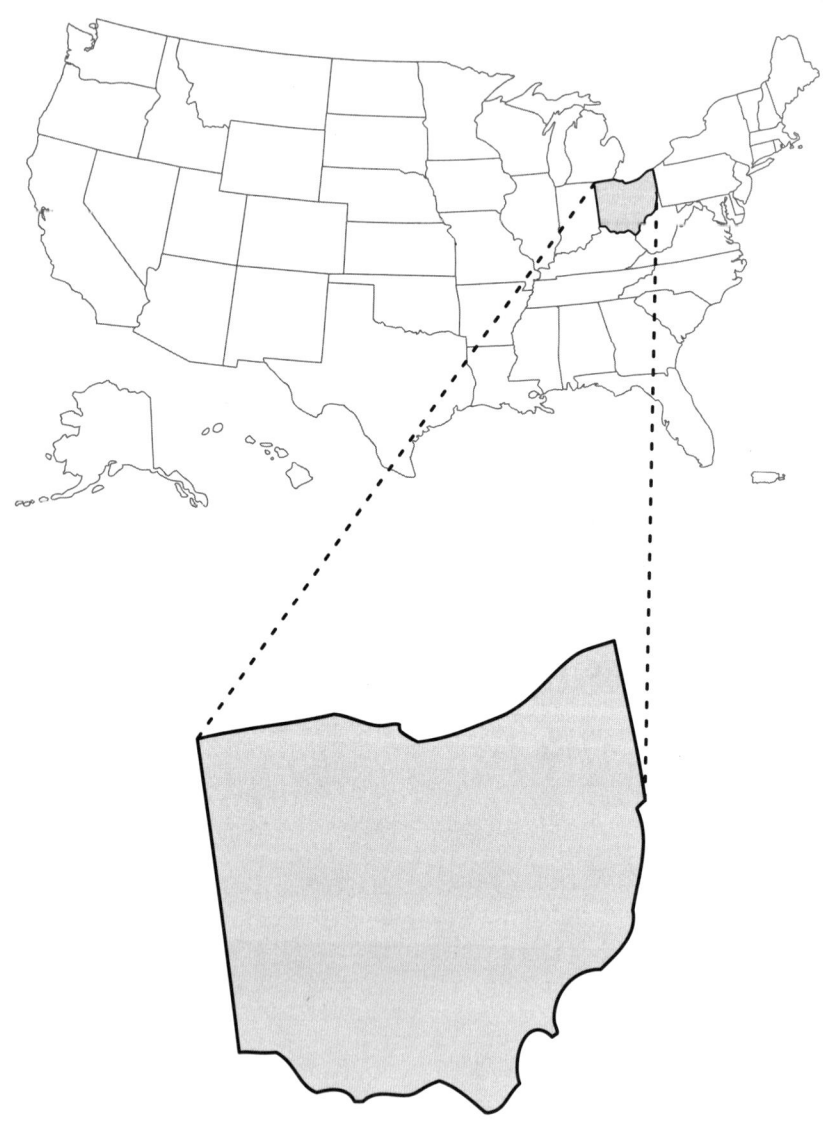

Where Is Ohio?

In the fall of 1770, George Washington took a trip down the Ohio River with a friend and some other men. They started at Fort Pitt, near what is today Pittsburgh, Pennsylvania, and went by canoe, a lightweight boat useful for steering through river waters. In some places, the Ohio River ran quickly, making it tricky to cross. Other times it flowed gently.

Washington watched the land go by from his canoe. Deer nibbled among beech and sycamore trees growing along the riverbanks. Wild geese and ducks swam nearby. Washington and his men caught catfish and hunted turkeys. They camped on shore during the night. Each day he wrote in his journal. The whole trip would take nine weeks, ending in what is now Kentucky.

On October 27, Washington's canoe passed the mouth of the Muskingum River. He looked out over the land and thought it would be good for farming. Years later, in 1788, Washington wrote to a friend about a new settlement near the Muskingum River. He said if he were a young man just starting out, there was no place he'd rather live than that area.

The settlement Washington wrote about was a town named Marietta. It was the first American town in the land that would become Ohio.

CHAPTER 1
The Great State of Ohio

Ohio's story begins with water. Indigenous people have made their homes in the land between Lake Erie and the Ohio River for more than fourteen thousand years. The Ohio River starts in Pennsylvania and ends in Illinois. Along the way, it runs through 451 miles of Ohio and makes up the state's southern boundary. Kentucky and West Virginia sit to Ohio's south and southeast. To the north, the state is bordered by Lake Erie, the fourth-largest Great Lake in North America. The state also neighbors Michigan, Pennsylvania, and Indiana.

Ohio has a humid, continental climate. That means its four seasons have different temperatures and bring plenty of rain and snow. Summers are hot, with highs in the mid-eighties to nineties. Winters are cold, and the temperature sometimes drops below freezing. The state is almost the same length north to south as it is east to west—about two hundred miles. Altogether, Ohio covers 44,825 square miles, making it the thirty-fourth-largest US state by area. The water that shaped all those miles—and formed the Ohio River and Lake Erie—arrived as ice!

The Pleistocene Epoch (say: ply-sto-seen Epock) was a period from 2.6 million years ago to 11,700 years ago. During that time, glaciers (huge areas of ice that stay frozen for hundreds or even thousands of years) moved in and out of what would become Ohio. One massive ice sheet covered two-thirds of the state. It was thousands of feet thick in some places! As the glaciers' heavy weight caused them to slide forward, they flattened the land almost everywhere. That's why plains (large areas of flat land) are the most common

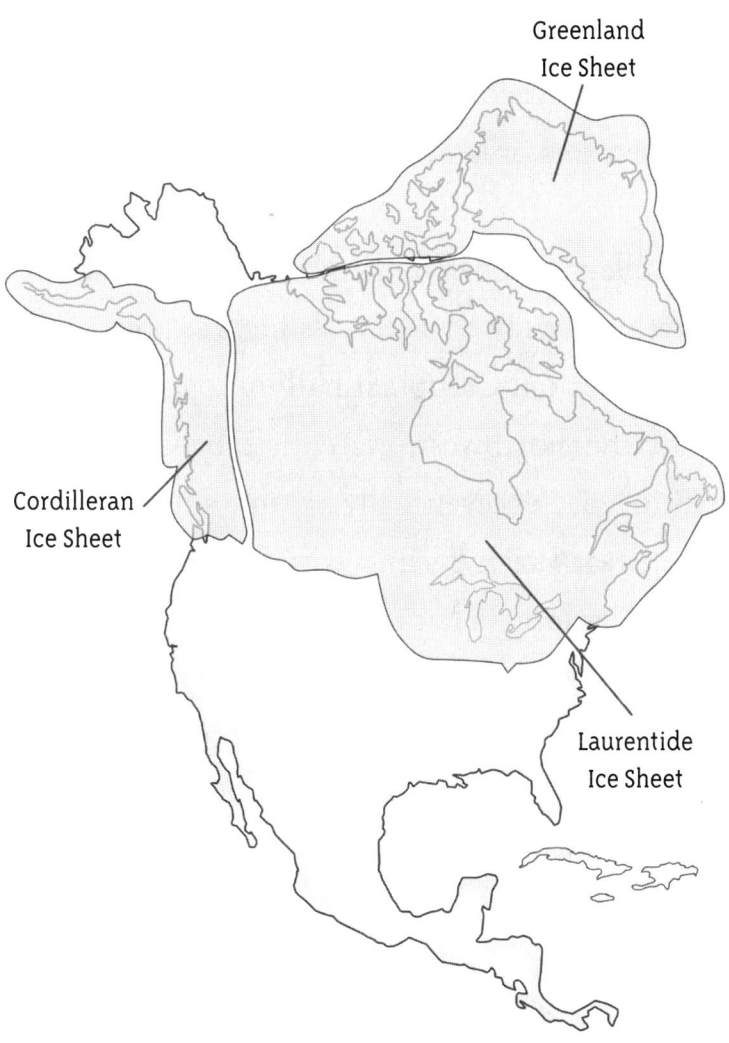

Greenland
Ice Sheet

Cordilleran
Ice Sheet

Laurentide
Ice Sheet

landform found in Ohio and cover nearly all of the state's western side. The glaciers stopped before they reached all of the Appalachian Plateau (a raised area of land that's flat on top) in the east and southeast, so that region kept some of its hills and valleys. Thanks to the glaciers, Ohio's average elevation is only 850 feet. Its highest point is the 1,550-foot-tall Campbell Hill in Logan County.

In the northwest, water left behind by the melting glaciers eventually became a huge swamp. The Great Black Swamp was 40 miles wide and 120 miles long. That's almost as big as the entire state of Connecticut! Beech, maple, and other trees grew in its murky water and created gloomy forests. Clouds of disease-carrying mosquitoes filled the swamp, often sickening those who tried to cross it.

In the 1850s, Ohioans worked to drain the Great Black Swamp. They cut down its trees and dug ditches that drew off water to dry it up. By the end of the nineteenth century, the swamp was gone. The soil that had been underwater was rich in nutrients and perfect for growing crops. What was once swamp became valuable farmland.

Draining the Great Black Swamp also meant that Ohio's largest natural wetland was gone. Ohio lost 90 percent of its wetlands when the swamp was destroyed. Today, people recognize that wetlands are a vital habitat for plants and animals that also help clean water that's held by the soil and rock underground, called groundwater. Ohio's Department of Natural Resources is now working to restore some of the state's wetlands.

Slow-moving glaciers also helped create the Ohio River, one of the state's most important ecosystems. (An ecosystem consists of the living and nonliving things in one area.) More than 160 species of fish are found in its waters, including bass, walleye, and catfish. Paddlefish also live there. This unique fish can weigh almost two

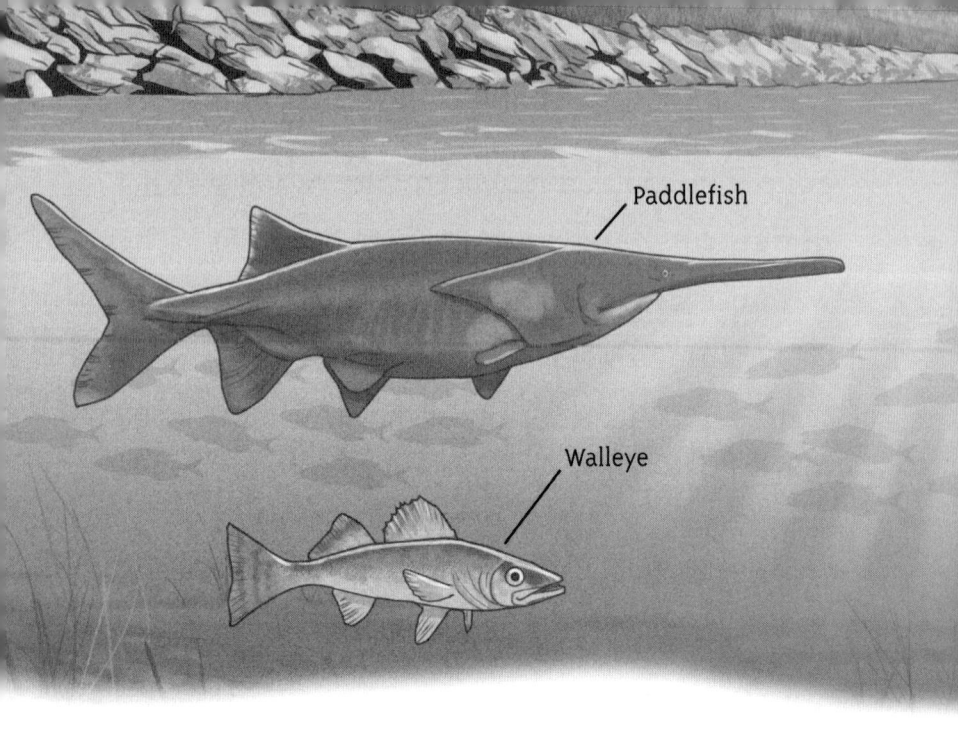

Paddlefish

Walleye

hundred pounds and first appeared fifty million years before the dinosaurs! Fish from the Ohio River become food for animals like otters and bald eagles. Migrating birds stop to rest along the river's banks. Its water provides for plants and animals as well as for millions of people.

The Ohio River isn't the state's only waterway. Ohio has more than sixty thousand streams, rivers, ponds, and lakes. In the north, glaciers carved out

Otter

Catfish

Bass

a basin (a bowl-shaped dip in Earth's surface) that filled with water and became Lake Erie. Ohio has about three hundred miles of shoreline on this Great Lake. Lake Erie is home to thousands of plant and animal species and is a source of valuable rocks and minerals like sandstone and salt. It also supplies water to millions of people. Lake Erie is an important natural resource for Ohio and has been for thousands of years.

The Hopewell Ceremonial Earthworks

Hopewell Culture is the term used to describe groups of people who lived in Ohio and eastern North America during the Middle Woodland Period (200 BCE–500 CE). We don't know what they called themselves, but they were probably made up of many nations. The Hopewell Culture built a series of enormous earthworks (piled-up banks of earth) in what is now southern and central Ohio between 1,600 and 2,000 years ago. These earthworks can still be seen today. The ring of soil called the Great Circle is so large that Egypt's Great Pyramid of Giza could sit inside it. Another, called Mound City, is made up of twenty-five mounds and stretches the length of ten football fields.

The earthworks were sacred gathering places, though we aren't sure what exactly went on there. We do know that peoples from across North America

traveled there to be together for ceremonies. They left artifacts made from mica, copper, and seashells.

In 2023, the Hopewell Ceremonial Earthworks were named a UNESCO World Heritage site. UNESCO stands for the United Nations Educational, Scientific, and Cultural Organization. Its goal is to protect important cultural places. The Hopewell Ceremonial Earthworks are the first World Heritage site in Ohio.

Shawnee, Miami, Lenape (say: la-NAH-pay), Ottawa, Wyandot (say: WHY-uhn-dot), and other Indigenous nations made their homes in Ohio. They hunted white-tailed deer, bison, elk, beavers, and more. (Today, bison and elk are no longer found in Ohio, but the white-tailed deer is the state mammal.) The animals were used for food and clothing, and also for trade. Ohio's forests provided wood to build their homes. They grew corn, squash, beans, fruit, and other crops, fished the rivers and streams, and built villages near the water.

Pickawillany (say: pick-uh-WILL-uh-nee) was one of those villages. In 1747, some members of the Miami Nation settled near the Great Miami River. They supplied English traders with furs. By 1750, about twelve hundred Miami people lived in Pickawillany. French traders were not happy that the villagers were working with the English instead of with them. In 1752, French soldiers, helped by a group of Ottawa, attacked the village. Pickawillany's leader was killed, and the rest of the villagers scattered.

It wouldn't be the last time the Miami and other Indigenous nations were chased out of their Ohio homes by Europeans.

CHAPTER 2
On the Edge of America

It was 1783. The Revolutionary War was over, and the American colonies had won their freedom from England. Still, the United States government had a problem: It had no money to pay the soldiers who had fought for the new country's freedom. What it did have was land.

The peace agreement with England gave the United States ownership of an area north and west of the Ohio River. This region was known as the Northwest Territory, and it covered about 265,000 square miles. That's bigger than all of France! Adding the Northwest Territory to the United States doubled the country's size.

To manage all that land, the United States government passed the Northwest Ordinance (a law created by a government) in 1787. It allowed parts of the territory to become states. (Ohio, Indiana, Illinois, Michigan, Wisconsin, and Minnesota would all be created from the Northwest Territory.) The Northwest Ordinance also made slavery illegal in the new territory and protected religious freedom and other rights.

The United States government gave its veterans (people who served in its army during the American Revolution) land in the Northwest Territory instead of money. It also sold land to make money. Rufus Putnam, a general in the Revolutionary War, saw an opportunity. He formed the Ohio Company of Associates. They made a deal with the government to buy a million and a half acres in the Northwest Territory. They wanted to establish Ohio's first town.

In 1787, forty-eight men set out from Massachusetts with Rufus Putnam as one of their leaders. The settlers brought axes, hoes, and other tools they needed to build a town. The side of the wagon that carried their belongings was painted with the words "For the Ohio." They walked seven hundred miles until they reached the start of the Ohio River in Pennsylvania. Then they built boats to take them the rest of the way. It was a long trip. On April 7, 1788, the settlers' boats

reached a spot where the Ohio River branched off into the smaller Muskingum River that would be their new home. It was the same place George Washington had seen from his canoe in 1770. They chose six thousand acres for the town and planned where streets, homes, stores, and fields for crops would go. Then they got to work.

At that time, as much as 95 percent of Ohio was covered by forests. Trees such as beech, oak, ash, and maple covered the land. Buckeye trees grew everywhere. (Today, the buckeye is the state tree. Ohio's nickname is "the Buckeye State.") The Ohio Company's settlers cut down trees and used the wood to build houses, barns, fences, and more. They also burned it to heat their homes and cook their food. Putnam and other members of the Ohio Company met to name their new town. They called it Marietta in honor of French queen Marie Antoinette. (The queen had supported the Americans during the Revolutionary War.) A week later, the Northwest Territory's first governor arrived. His name was Arthur St. Clair.

More settlers came. John Cleves Symmes, a New Jersey judge and congressman, and his partners bought more than three hundred thousand acres in southwest Ohio to resell to settlers. Twenty-four men and eleven families

Settlers cutting down a buckeye tree.

traveled down the Ohio River to establish Losantiville, which would be renamed Cincinnati two years later. A group of six hundred people from France settled downriver from Marietta. Altogether, more than ten thousand people moved to Ohio during 1788 and 1789.

The Northwest Ordinance promised that the Shawnee, Miami, and other nations would not be forced to give up their land. Land-hungry settlers ignored it and moved into Indigenous territory, and nothing was done by the United States government to defend the rules of the Northwest Ordinance. The Miami, Shawnee, Delaware, and other nations came together in the Western Confederacy and fought back. In 1790, President George Washington ordered that United States soldiers stop them. Warriors led by Miami leader Little Turtle and Shawnee leader Blue Jacket defeated US soldiers in battles in northern and southern Ohio over the next year.

George Washington put Anthony Wayne in charge. Wayne had been a successful general during the Revolutionary War. To defeat the Western Confederacy, he trained five thousand soldiers and marched them into Ohio. On August 20, 1794, Wayne and about three thousand of his troops met a thousand warriors in a clearing where

Little Turtle
(Mihšihkinaahkwa in
the Miami language)

Blue Jacket
(Weyapiersenwah in
the Shawnee language)

trees had been knocked down by a tornado, near what is now Toledo. In less than an hour, the US soldiers won the Battle of Fallen Timbers.

The loss made the Western Confederacy realize they were outnumbered. Anthony Wayne and the leaders of the Western Confederacy met in 1795 to work out a peace agreement. Leaders of the Miami, Shawnee, Wyandot, Ottawa, and other nations felt they had no choice but to sign the Treaty of Greenville, which took almost all of Ohio from them and gave it to the settlers. Many Indigenous people were forced out or left Ohio on their own. Others stayed, but the United States government no longer recorded them as being Indigenous in its population data.

After the Treaty of Greenville, Ohio was seen as available for settlement by Americans (which did not include Indigenous people). The United States government opened offices to sell land and priced it cheaply to appeal to settlers from other parts of the young country. People in Rhode Island, Connecticut, and Massachusetts had run out of places to build and farm. They heard that Ohio land was flat and easy to clear. Its rich soil was good for growing corn, grains, and other crops. Settlers got "Ohio Fever" and poured in.

CHAPTER 3
Becoming the Buckeye State

By 1801, 45,000 people lived in the Northwest Territory (the area northwest of the Ohio River). Thomas Worthington was a member of the territorial government. He believed Ohio was ready to be a state.

Worthington asked President Thomas Jefferson and the US Congress to approve his idea officially, even though there weren't enough people living in Ohio yet. (The Northwest Ordinance said a territory needed to have 60,000 people to become a state. Ohio had around 45,000.) Jefferson agreed. In 1802, the president approved an act that said that Ohio could create a state constitution. As soon as Ohio had a constitution, Congress could vote to make it a state.

Ohio's constitutional convention met in Chillicothe in 1802. When the state constitution was finished, Worthington took it to Congress. They voted yes, and Ohio became the seventeenth US state on March 1, 1803. Chillicothe became Ohio's first capital. Later, Thomas Worthington became the state's sixth governor. Today, he is remembered as the "Father of Ohio Statehood."

Ohio kept growing. In the 1800s, more than 80 percent of Ohioans lived on farms, where they raised lots of corn and wheat. The land was not only good for crops but also for raising hogs. In the 1820s, Cincinnati was nicknamed "Porkopolis" because it prepared as many as 30,000 hogs for market per year!

In the mid-1800s, German and Irish people moved to Ohio in search of jobs and land. Many settled in Cincinnati, Cleveland, and Columbus. Ohio's immigrants helped build the state's canals, railroads, farms, and cities. They also dug coal

from the ground in the eastern and southern parts of the state, and Ohio coal was sold around the United States as a source of heat for homes and fuel for boats, trains, and factories.

The members of Ohio's General Assembly decided they wanted a new capital city near the middle of the state. In 1812, plans were laid out to build that capital—Columbus. In 1862, the US government passed an act that set aside land

for colleges and universities. The Ohio General Assembly voted to build a college in Columbus in 1870, and it became the home of the Ohio Agricultural and Mechanical College. In 1878, its name was changed to The Ohio State University.

Boats steamed up and down the Ohio River, carrying crops, meat, and coal to market. Cincinnati was a major hub for trade along the river and became known as "the Queen of the

West." In 1827, the Ohio and Erie Canal opened, which connected Lake Erie with the Ohio River. Cleveland, built on the shores of Lake Erie, became a center for loading and unloading goods transported across its waters. It was nicknamed "the City of Light" in 1879 when a local inventor named Charles Brush lit its public square with the first outdoor electric lights in the United States.

Ohio was a free state. That meant slavery was against the law, though Black people still faced racism and laws that limited their rights. Black settlers moved to Ohio and built communities throughout the state in the 1800s. Carthagena, one of the largest, had more than six hundred families. By 1860, almost thirty-seven thousand Black Americans lived in Ohio. In 1879, George Washington Williams became the first Black American elected to Ohio's legislature.

In the years leading up to the Civil War, the Ohio River was the boundary between the free states and the southern states where slavery was allowed. Ohio became an important stop on the Underground Railroad, the network of safe houses and secret routes that helped enslaved Black people escape to safety in Canada. It was against the law to help a person escape slavery, even in a free state, so the people on the Underground Railroad used codes. A conductor was someone who helped guide freedom seekers, and an agent was a person who helped hide them. Ohio had more than fifteen hundred conductors and agents.

John Parker, a formerly enslaved Black man, was a conductor in Ripley, Ohio. He was an inventor by day and a conductor by night. He

helped more than one thousand people escape slavery. Experts think that agents and conductors like Parker helped between forty and fifty thousand freedom seekers through Ohio. That's almost half of all the people who were able to escape slavery before the Civil War.

John Parker leading freedom seekers to safety

By 1900, Ohio's population had grown to more than four million people. Railroads replaced steamboats, although barges still carried some goods on the Ohio River. The Flood of 1913 destroyed the Ohio and Erie Canal, and it was not rebuilt. The state continued to produce many crops, but more Ohioans left farms for cities as industry (businesses that change raw materials into goods) increased. Ohio's factories produced iron and steel. Large amounts of underground rock salt helped the state become the third-largest salt producer in the United States. Its sandstone was used in buildings, and its sand and gravel helped build roads around the nation. Even the land of Ohio was changing: By 1920, nearly all of Ohio's hardwood trees had been cleared for farming or exported as lumber.

The state would continue to change in the years to come. Even more factories opened to turn Ohio's iron ore (rock that holds a valuable substance) into steel. Steel is one of the world's most used metals, and Youngstown and Cleveland became major steel-making centers. Akron was nicknamed "the Rubber Capital of the World" when six different rubber-making companies based their headquarters there to produce tires, garden hoses, and more. In 1959, the Great Lakes–St. Lawrence Seaway opened. This waterway connects the Great Lakes to the Atlantic Ocean and made it possible to ship even more US goods overseas. Toledo and Cleveland became busy ports on the seaway.

People flocked to the new jobs. Thousands of Black Americans moved to Cleveland, Cincinnati, and Columbus from the southern states. Struggling farmers left the Appalachian region to find work in Akron. People from Eastern Europe also immigrated to Ohio. Suburbs (places to live outside a city) grew as new roads made it possible for people to live away from the city and drive in for work or visits.

Ohio's workers faced new challenges when other countries began producing cheaper steel, and some of the state's steel-making factories closed. In the 1980s, Ohio lost about half its steel industry jobs. Akron's rubber industry also suffered when a French company made a new, more popular kind of tire. Some companies were able to make changes and stay in business—Cleveland-Cliffs is the biggest producer of flat-rolled steel in the US, and Goodyear Tire still has its headquarters in Akron. E. E. Ward Moving and Storage Company in Columbus, Ohio, survived all of the 1900s and is still a moving company today. It is the oldest African American–owned business in the United States that has never stopped operating.

Some big companies and well-known brands got their start in Ohio. Goodyear Tire was originally a bicycle tire company. In 1897, J. M. Smucker sold apple butter from a horse-drawn carriage in a small Ohio town, launching the company that now makes jelly, Jif peanut butter, and more. Cincinnati's Procter & Gamble sold Ivory soap for the first time in the 1800s and now has hundreds of products. Life Savers candy was invented by a Cleveland chocolate maker. Comic book character Superman was even dreamed up in Cleveland! Every day, people all over the world use and enjoy things that started out in the great state of Ohio.

CHAPTER 4
The Heart of It All

More than eleven million people now live in cities, suburbs, towns, and farms across Ohio. Columbus is the state's largest city—over 900,000 people live there! Almost 5 percent of the people living in Ohio are immigrants from other countries, with most new Ohioans moving there from India, Mexico, and China. Central Ohio has also welcomed about 45,000 refugees from Somalia in the past ten years.

Agriculture is still one of Ohio's largest industries and contributes over $124 billion to the state's economy every year. Ohio has about 75,000 farms, almost all owned by families. Ohio's farmers make more than two hundred kinds of products, including more Swiss cheese than any other state.

Ohio is also one of the country's top producers of eggs, tomatoes, pumpkins, bell peppers, and sweet corn. Hundreds of Ohio companies pack and ship food around the United States.

About 194,000 Ohioans make vehicles, plastics, parts for airplanes, and more. The state is the leading US producer of soap, paint, and cleaning products sold to other countries. Ohio is also looking to the future, building solar panels and parts for robots.

Industry has caused some challenges in Ohio. Today, less than 30 percent of the state still has forests, and factories and railroads dumped so much pollution and oil into the Cuyahoga River that it caught fire in 1969. (It wasn't the first time. The river had caught fire more than ten times in the previous one hundred years.) Newspapers and magazines around the country featured the Cuyahoga River Fire, and it became a symbol of the problems caused by pollution. The attention paid to the fire helped lead to the first Earth Day and the forming of the Environmental Protection Agency. Water pollution is still a concern, but there are many groups working to keep Ohio's water clean.

Many of the state's waterways are great places to have fun! Sandy beaches cover parts of Lake Erie's shore, and visitors can take a ferry to Put-in-Bay, a small town on South Bass Island. Kayakers and boaters enjoy Ohio's lakes and can even use maps to follow water trails. Some, such as the Great Miami River Water Trail, are popular with people who like to fish.

For more outdoor fun, Ohio has one national park, the Cuyahoga Valley National Park, plus seventy-five state parks with thousands of miles of trails. Hikers may catch a glimpse of Ohio's state reptile, the black racer snake, or spot the red feathers of a cardinal, the state bird. Hocking Hills is one of the most popular state parks.

Millions of people visit its waterfalls, cliffs, and caves every year.

Ohio is considered the birthplace of two professional sports—baseball and football. The Cincinnati Red Stockings, now known as the Cincinnati Reds, were the nation's first known pro baseball team and have won five World Series. (The Cleveland Guardians are Ohio's other Major League Baseball team.) The National

Football League was formed in Canton, and the Pro Football Hall of Fame was built there. Ohio has two pro football teams—the Cincinnati Bengals and the Cleveland Browns. High school and college football games are also popular with fans. The Ohio State Buckeyes played for the first time more than one hundred years ago and have won nine national championships since then.

LeBron James brought another championship

to Ohio. He spent eleven seasons playing basketball with the Cleveland Cavaliers and led the team to an NBA title in 2016. James grew up in Akron and still supports the city. In 2018, he founded a school there. Basketball star Stephen Curry was also born in Akron!

One of Ohio's nicknames is "the Birthplace of Aviation" because Orville and Wilbur Wright, inventors who worked on some of the earliest airplanes, grew up in Dayton. The Wright brothers aren't the state's only connection to aviation (the flying or operating of aircraft). Ohioan John Glenn set a speed record for a cross-country flight as a test pilot and was the first American to orbit Earth. Neil Armstrong, another Ohioan, was the first person to walk on the moon. The state is also home to the world's largest military air and space museum, the National Museum of the United States Air Force, at Wright-Patterson Air Force Base, near Dayton. Visitors can see more than

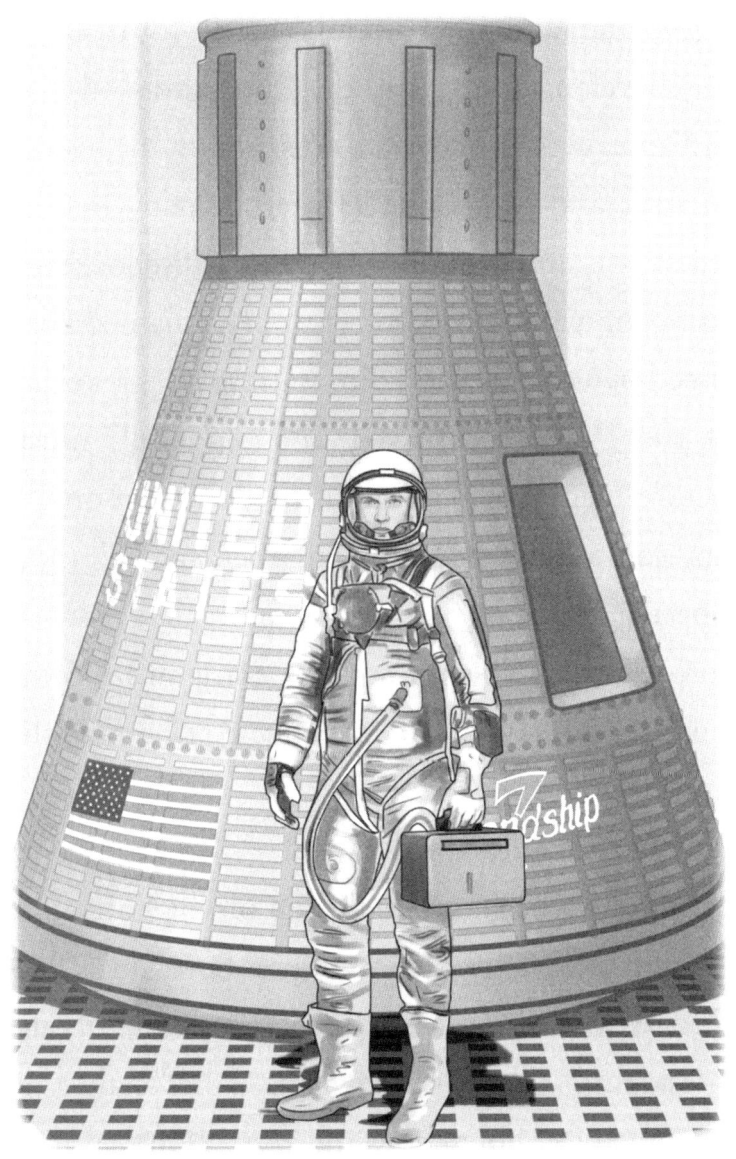

John Glenn

350 planes and other aircraft there—for free!

Cleveland is home to the Rock and Roll Hall of Fame, which includes a museum on the history of rock and roll music as well as many famous musicians and producers. A DJ (or disc jockey— someone who selects songs to play) named Alan Freed worked at a radio station in Cleveland in the 1950s. He played "rock and roll" music before many people were using that term on TV and radio. His role in making rock and roll more popular is one of the reasons the Hall of Fame is in Cleveland. The museum's opening in 1996 was honored by visits from stars like Aretha Franklin and Bob Dylan.

Ohio is also nicknamed "the Mother of Presidents" because seven out of the forty-four United States presidents were born in Ohio. Today, when it comes to choosing United States presidents, Ohio is known as a bellwether, or a state that shows how the rest of the country will vote. When a person running for president wins Ohio, chances are they'll win the election. Ohioans have voted for the winner in all but three presidential elections since 1900. That's why there's an expression that says "As Ohio goes, so goes the nation."

Ohio began as an important gathering place, and has remained that way for thousands of years. Its waters and land have been home to Indigenous nations and settlers. It was once the edge of the newly formed United States. In the early twenty-first century, nearly half of the United States population was located within five hundred miles of Columbus. As the slogan says, Ohio truly is the heart of it all.

Ohio at a Glance

Statehood: 1803

Nickname: The Buckeye State

Abbreviation: OH

State Motto: With God, all things are possible

State Tree: Buckeye

State Animal: White-tailed deer

Capital: Columbus

Size: 44,825 square miles

Population: Over 11 million

Famous People from Ohio:

Tecumseh (Shawnee leader), Thomas Edison (inventor), Toni Morrison (author), Steven Spielberg (movie director), Simone Biles (Olympic gymnast)

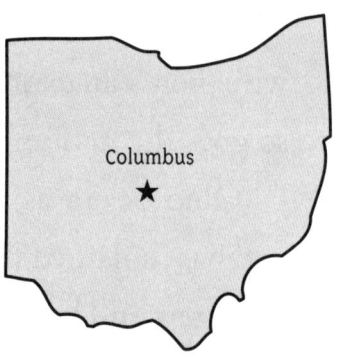

Columbus ★

State flag

State bird
Cardinal

State flower
Red carnation

FUN FACT:
Ohio has more than 13 million acres
of farmland. That's a little more than
half of all the land in the state!

Timeline of Ohio

1–400 CE	The Hopewell Ceremonial Earthworks are built
1788	Ohio Company settlers establish Marietta, the first American town of the Northwest Territory
1795	The Treaty of Greenville forces Indigenous nations to give up almost all their claims to Ohio land
1803	Ohio becomes the seventeenth US state
1812	Planning begins for the future state capital, Columbus
1840	Carthagena, a community of Black Americans, is founded
1843	The Underground Railroad operates for the first time in Ohio
1865	The American Civil War ends
1870	The Ohio State University is founded in Columbus
1879	Cleveland becomes the first US city with public outdoor electric lights
1920	The National Football League is founded in Canton
1969	Neil Armstrong walks on the moon
2023	The Hopewell Ceremonial Earthworks become a UNESCO World Heritage Site

Timeline of the World

2550 BCE	Building begins on the Great Pyramid of Giza
1791 CE	Congress adds the Bill of Rights to the Constitution
1795	Ludwig van Beethoven makes his public debut in Vienna
1810	Mexico declares its independence from Spain
1820	European explorers spot Antarctica for the first time
1854	The Treaty of Kanagawa is signed, opening up trade between Japan and the United States
1889	Construction of the Eiffel Tower in Paris is completed
1903	The United States acquires the rights to build and operate the Panama Canal
1928	Penicillin is discovered
1963	Martin Luther King Jr. gives his "I Have a Dream" speech
1990	The Hubble Space Telescope is launched
1994	China begins to build Three Gorges Dam
2023	India passes China as the country with the most people in the world
2024	The thirty-third Summer Olympic Games are held in Paris

Bibliography

*Books for young readers

*Buckley, James, Jr. *Who Were the Wright Brothers?* New York: Penguin Workshop, 2014.

*Dean, Tanya West, and W. David Speas. *Along the Ohio Trail: A Short History of Ohio Lands*. Columbus, Ohio: Auditor of State, 2003. https://ohioauditor.gov/publications/docs/AlongTheOhioTrail.pdf.

*Edwards, Roberta. *Who Was Neil Armstrong?* New York: Penguin Workshop, 2008.

*Hubbard, Crystal. *Who Is LeBron James?* New York: Penguin Workshop, 2023.

Knepper, George W. *The Official Ohio Lands Book*. Columbus, Ohio: Auditor of State, 2002. https://ohioauditor.gov/publications/docs/OhioLandsBook.pdf.

"Ohio." *Britannica Kids*. https://kids.britannica.com/kids/article/Ohio/345513.

"Ohio." *National Geographic Kids*. https://kids.nationalgeographic.com/geography/states/article/ohio.

*Saxton, Anne. *Ohio.* Minneapolis: Abdo Publishing, 2023.

*Stille, Darlene R. *Ohio*. America the Beautiful. Third Series. New York: Scholastic Inc., 2014.